MORMON
FOR
GEN Z

Andrew Cooper

The Old And New Testament Mormon For Gen Z

———◆———

———◆———

CONTENTS

Lehi's Vision:
A Message for Today

(1 Nephi 1)

Lehi's Vision:
A Message for Today
(1 Nephi 1)

———◆ ◆———

Around 600 B.C., in ancient Jerusalem, Lehi lived in a time of social upheaval, not unlike the challenges we face today. Amidst this, he sought understanding through deep contemplation, leading to a life-changing vision.

One evening, without the distractions of modern technology, Lehi received what we might call a 'divine notification.' He saw a pillar of fire, a symbol so intense it sparked both awe and fear. This wasn't your everyday dream; it was a cosmic alert about Jerusalem's impending doom due to its societal decay—paralleling our current global issues like environmental crisis and social injustice.

Yet, the vision also offered hope, introducing the concept of a Messiah who'd bring salvation. This message is timeless, reminding us that in our darkest hours, there's always a beacon of hope.

Lehi's response? To share this revelation, advocating for change. However, much like today's activists who often face backlash, Lehi's warnings were met with hostility, leading to his and his family's exile—a journey towards new beginnings.

For Generation Z, Lehi's story underscores the importance of staying woke to the world's realities while holding onto hope for a better future. It's a call to action, inspiring us to reflect deeply and perhaps, find our own pillar of fire in the quest for truth and change.

———◆ ◆———

Lehi's Family Odyssey: A Desert Saga

(1 Nephi 2-18))

Lehi's Family Odyssey:
A Desert Saga

(1 Nephi 2-18)

Imagine making a choice that uproots your entire life, pushing you and your family into the unknown. This was the reality for Lehi and his family, who embarked on an epic journey not by choice but by necessity, guided by visions and a promise of a new land. Their desert trek was more than a physical journey; it was a test of faith, patience, and family bonds.

Lehi's family faced the harsh realities of wilderness life, where water was scarce, food was uncertain, and the path forward was unclear. Every step was a leap of faith. Imagine trading the comfort of your home for the unpredictability of the wild, where every convenience you've ever known is stripped away. It's like going off the grid, but not as a digital detox by choice—rather, as a survival imperative.

This journey was marked by moments of profound spiritual insight and daunting challenges. They had to learn to live off the land, with Nephi and his brothers occasionally returning to Jerusalem for supplies and guidance, each trip increasing their risks and challenges. The dynamics within Lehi's family mirror the complexities of modern family life, where disagreements and reconciliations shape relationships, teaching us lessons about love, forgiveness, and resilience.

For Generation Z, Lehi's odyssey is a metaphor for the journey of life. It reflects the uncertainties of stepping into adulthood, the complexities of family dynamics, and the search for personal and collective purpose. It teaches that growth often comes from discomfort and that faith can guide us through life's deserts to find our promised lands.

Their desert saga also emphasizes the importance of environmental stewardship, a timely reminder of our responsibility to care for the Earth. It's a call to action for young people to lead the way in sustainable living, respecting and preserving the natural world for future generations.

In essence, Lehi's family journey through the desert offers rich lessons in faith, perseverance, and the transformative power of embarking on the unknown. It's a story that inspires courage to face the wildernesses in our lives, armed with hope and a sense of purpose.

Nephi's Mission:
The Brass Plates
(1 Nephi 3-4)

Nephi's Mission: The Brass Plates

(1 Nephi 3-4)

In a narrative that feels like a mix between a spy thriller and a quest for ancient wisdom, we find Nephi, a young man determined to follow a divine command, even when the odds are stacked against him. The mission? To retrieve the brass plates, essential records held by a powerful and unyielding man, Laban, in Jerusalem.

Imagine being asked to get the most exclusive, guarded content—not for clout or likes but because it holds the key to your people's history and future enlightenment. That's the task Nephi faced, underscoring a journey of faith, strategy, and unwavering resolve.

Despite initial failures and serious risks, including the potential for violence and the reality of family conflict, Nephi steps up. He doesn't have a detailed plan but moves forward with faith, embodying the Gen Z ethos of improvisation and adaptability in the face of challenges.

The turning point comes when Nephi, after two failed attempts and considerable personal risk, finds Laban incapacitated. Faced with a moral dilemma that would leave anyone questioning their next move, Nephi chooses to follow what he believes is divine guidance, securing the plates. It's a moment of intense decision-making, reflecting the complex choices today's youth often face, where the right path isn't always clear.

Retrieving the brass plates isn't just about accomplishing a task; it's about securing a legacy and wisdom for generations to come. It highlights the value of knowledge, history, and cultural continuity, themes that resonate deeply in our era of information overload and quest for identity.

Nephi's story teaches us about the importance of courage, conviction, and the sometimes murky path to doing what's right. It's a call to value our roots and stories, to stand up for what we believe in, even when the journey is fraught with uncertainty and danger.

In the modern context, Nephi's adventure is a powerful reminder that sometimes, achieving something greater requires stepping out of our comfort zones, facing our fears, and making tough decisions. It's about the quest for something that transcends immediate gratification—a lesson in persistence, faith, and the pursuit of a higher purpose.

The Vision of the Tree of Life: A Journey to Meaning

(I Nephi 8, 11)

The Vision of the Tree of Life: A Journey to Meaning

(1 Nephi 8, 11)

In an immersive vision that transcends time, Lehi finds himself in a dark and dreary wilderness, a metaphor for the confusion and challenges that often cloud our path to understanding and purpose. As he navigates this daunting landscape, he discovers a radiant tree, its white fruit promising happiness and fulfillment. This vision of the Tree of Life becomes a profound exploration of life's journey, highlighting the significance of love, connection, and the pursuit of true joy.

Imagine navigating the complexities of today's world, where paths are many, and distractions abound. Lehi's vision speaks to the heart of Generation Z, living in an era where the quest for authenticity and meaning often clashes with the noise of social media and societal expectations. The vision is a reminder that amidst life's chaos, there exists a path leading to pure joy, symbolized by the tree's divine fruit.

The journey to the tree is fraught with obstacles. A river of water represents the hardships and temptations that can lead us astray, while a mist of darkness symbolizes the confusion and doubts that obscure our vision. The iron rod along the path to the tree stands as a symbol of steadfastness in faith and truth, guiding us through life's uncertainties.

Lehi's vision is not just his own; it becomes a shared experience with his family, each member's reaction reflecting their individual struggles and desires. This collective journey underscores the importance of family and community in our quest for understanding and fulfillment. It highlights that while our paths may diverge, our shared experiences and support for one another are invaluable.

For Generation Z, this vision offers a rich tapestry of symbolism applicable to the modern quest for identity and purpose. It encourages a reevaluation of what truly matters—emphasizing not the ephemeral pleasures highlighted by likes and follows but the deeper, enduring joy found in love, meaningful connections, and the pursuit of light in our lives.

Nephi's Glimpse into the Future: Nations and Destiny

(1 Nephi 11-14)

Nephi's Glimpse into the Future: Nations and Destiny

(1 Nephi 11-14)

Nephi's vision, an expansive panorama spanning the rise and fall of civilizations, is more than a historical preview—it's a deep dive into the consequences of human actions and the persistent hope that faith offers. As Nephi is taken on a spiritual journey through time, he witnesses not only the future of his own descendants but also the coming of Jesus Christ to the Americas, the establishment and struggle of early Christian churches, and the eventual fate of nations across the world.

This narrative is particularly resonant for Generation Z, a group deeply concerned with the trajectory of human society and the planet. Nephi sees the beauty of human connection and the devastation of conflict, mirroring today's global challenges. From climate change to social injustices, the vision outlines the duality of human potential for both creation and destruction.

Nephi's vision emphasizes the role of faith and the impact of choices on societal outcomes. He observes the spread of Christ's teachings and how they shape societies, pointing to the enduring influence of spiritual values across ages. This aspect of his vision encourages young readers to consider their actions and beliefs' long-term effects on the world's moral and ethical fabric.

Moreover, Nephi witnesses the formation of a great and abominable church, symbolizing the corruption and loss of spiritual truths that lead societies astray. This part of the vision serves as a warning against the perils of power and greed, urging Generation Z to strive for authenticity and integrity in their personal and collective pursuits.

The vision also offers hope, showcasing the restoration of the Gospel and the gathering of people to truth and righteousness. It's a testament to the enduring nature of truth and the potential for renewal and healing, inspiring young individuals to be agents of positive change in their communities.

For Generation Z, Nephi's vision of the future nations is not just a prophecy but a call to action. It's an invitation to engage with the world thoughtfully, to champion causes that promote peace and understanding, and to contribute to a legacy of compassion and resilience. This narrative empowers young readers to envision a future where, despite challenges, the light of hope and the power of collective action can lead to a more just and compassionate world.

Nephi's Test of Faith: Crafting a New Bow

(1 Nephi 16)

Nephi's Test of Faith: Crafting a New Bow

(1 Nephi 16)

In a moment that could easily belong to a modern tale of survival and ingenuity, Nephi finds himself facing a critical challenge. His family, already struggling in the harsh wilderness, encounters a dire situation when Nephi's bow, a key tool for their survival, breaks. This setback isn't just a physical hurdle; it's a test of faith, resilience, and the ability to innovate under pressure.

For Generation Z, accustomed to a world where solutions are often a click away, Nephi's predicament underscores the value of self-reliance and the creative problem-solving that defines entrepreneurial spirit. When the familiar paths to sustenance and success are blocked, how do you adapt? Nephi answers this by turning to the resources at hand, not in despair, but with determination to forge a new path forward.

Constructing a new bow from the materials available in the wilderness, Nephi demonstrates an essential lesson in adaptability and perseverance. His action is a testament to the idea that when traditional methods fail, innovation and a willingness to try new approaches are crucial. This story resonates with the young generation facing an uncertain future, emphasizing that flexibility and a proactive attitude can turn challenges into opportunities.

Nephi's reliance on faith through prayer before undertaking his task illustrates another critical lesson: the balance between divine guidance and personal effort. It's a reminder that while seeking spiritual support, tangible actions are necessary to achieve our goals. This balance between faith and works, between divine inspiration and human initiative, speaks directly to the hearts of young people navigating their journey, emphasizing that both elements are essential in the pursuit of success and fulfillment.

Moreover, Nephi's experience highlights the importance of contribution to the community. His efforts were not solely for personal gain but to sustain his family. It's a powerful message about the role of individuals in supporting and uplifting those around them, reinforcing the value of empathy, cooperation, and collective well-being.

Nephi Builds a Ship: Crafting the Future

(1 Nephi 17-18)

Nephi Builds a Ship:
Crafting the Future

(1 Nephi 17-18)

In an epic tale of innovation and determination, Nephi is tasked with something that seems impossible: building a ship to carry his family to an unknown land. Picture this as the ultimate DIY project, but instead of browsing YouTube for tutorials, Nephi's guidance comes through faith and divine inspiration.

This story hits differently for Gen Z, a generation known for valuing sustainability, innovation, and problem-solving. Nephi, without prior shipbuilding experience, embodies the quintessential innovator's spirit. He doesn't let skepticism from his brothers or his own uncertainties deter him. Instead, he leans into the challenge, driven by a vision of a better future for his family.

Nephi's process of building the ship is not just about physical construction but also about building trust, faith, and unity within his family. He faces mockery and doubt, especially from his brothers, who can't see the vision he's working towards. Yet, Nephi persists, using tools provided by the Lord and his own ingenuity to create something extraordinary.

This narrative is more than a historical account; it's a metaphor for the journey of creation and innovation that speaks to young minds today. It's about taking on environmental and societal challenges with a blend of faith in divine guidance and trust in our capabilities.

Nephi's story underscores the importance of resilience and adaptability, qualities that resonate with a generation facing an uncertain future. It teaches that breakthroughs often come not from external sources but from within, from the strength of our convictions and the courage to act on them.

As Nephi's ship finally takes to the sea, it's a testament to what can be achieved with a blend of divine inspiration and human effort. This journey across the waters is not just a physical relocation; it's a leap into the unknown, driven by hope and the belief in a promised future.

For Generation Z, Nephi's shipbuilding endeavor is a powerful reminder that facing daunting challenges with innovation and faith can lead us to new horizons. It's about harnessing our potential to create, lead, and inspire change, making a tangible impact on our world and charting a course towards a promising future.

The Promised Land: Blessings and Curses

(2 Nephi 1)

The Promised Land: Blessings and Curses

(2 Nephi 1)

In a poignant farewell address, Lehi speaks to his family, gathered around him in a new land far from their origins. This isn't just any land; it's a promised land, laden with potential and divine assurances. Yet, these promises come with a caveat: blessings for obedience and curses for disobedience. This principle isn't just ancient history; it's a timeless truth, echoing the modern understanding that our actions and choices significantly impact our environment and society.

For Generation Z, living in an era marked by climate change, social inequality, and a quest for justice, Lehi's message resonates profoundly. It frames the earth as a gift, one that requires stewardship and respect, where the collective choices of humanity determine the health and prosperity of the land and its inhabitants. It's a call to action, urging young individuals to live responsibly, not just for their sake but for the welfare of all generations to come.

Lehi's discourse highlights the interconnectedness of spiritual and temporal well-being, suggesting that the ethical and moral choices we make are inseparable from the physical health of our planet. This notion challenges Gen Z to consider how their values and actions align with the broader implications for society and the environment. It encourages a holistic approach to life, where sustainability, equity, and compassion are not just ideals but practical, everyday practices.

Furthermore, the promised land narrative invites reflection on the concept of "promised lands" in our lives—spaces of opportunity, growth, and potential. It reminds young people that while such spaces exist, their true value and the fulfillment of their promise depend on our commitment to principles of righteousness, community, and respect for the divine laws governing nature and human relations.

Lehi's address, therefore, is not just a historical or religious lesson; it's a metaphor for the contemporary world. It underlines the reality that our planet, our "promised land," hangs in the balance, with its future contingent on our collective decisions and actions. It's a sobering reminder of the responsibility we hold but also a message of hope. By choosing wisely and acting with foresight and compassion, we can secure blessings not just for ourselves but for the earth and all its inhabitants.

For Generation Z, the message is clear: the legacy they inherit and pass on will be defined by their respect for the earth, their commitment to justice, and their willingness to live in harmony with the divine and natural laws. The promised land's blessings are within reach, contingent on the choices made today.

Lehi's Blessing to Jacob: Lessons of Opposition and Choice

(2 Nephi 2)

Lehi's Blessing to Jacob: Lessons of Opposition and Choice

(2 Nephi 2)

In a deeply moving and philosophical discourse, Lehi imparts wisdom to his son Jacob, offering insights that transcend their immediate context and resonate with the very essence of human experience. At the heart of Lehi's blessing is the exploration of life's dualities—joy and pain, good and evil, freedom and constraint. These concepts aren't just abstract notions; they're the fabric of our daily lives, especially poignant for Generation Z, navigating a world of contrasts and seeking balance amidst chaos.

Lehi elucidates the necessity of opposition in all things, a principle that underscores the value of experiencing life's full spectrum. For young people today, who often grapple with the pressure to present a curated, flawless version of life on social media, this teaching offers a counter-narrative. It validates the whole range of human emotions and experiences, emphasizing that challenges, failures, and hardships are not just inevitable but essential for growth, empathy, and genuine joy.

This narrative speaks directly to the Gen Z ethos of authenticity and acceptance, encouraging a holistic embrace of life's complexities. It's a reminder that the pursuit of happiness isn't about the absence of difficulty but the presence of choice. Lehi's wisdom highlights the empowering principle of agency—the ability to choose our path, learn from our experiences, and ultimately shape our destiny.

Moreover, Lehi delves into the concepts of freedom and redemption, tying them to the essential role of the Messiah. This message of hope and liberation is particularly resonant in today's climate of social and personal striving for freedom and justice. It reassures young individuals of the inherent worth of every soul and the availability of divine grace, encouraging them to seek a path of compassion, service, and self-improvement.

Lehi's blessing to Jacob is more than a father's advice; it's a blueprint for navigating life with wisdom and resilience. It encourages Generation Z to embrace life's oppositions as avenues for growth, to exercise their moral agency with integrity, and to engage in the ongoing quest for understanding and purpose. In a world often seen in black and white, Lehi's words are a reminder of the richness of life's full spectrum and the transformative power of making choices rooted in love and truth.

For young readers, this message is a call to action—not to shun life's challenges but to face them with courage, knowing that each choice shapes not only their destiny but the world around them. It's an invitation to live fully, embracing the complex beauty of existence and contributing to a legacy of wisdom, compassion, and enduring joy.

The Division of the Nephites and Lamanites:
A Lesson in Identity and Destiny

(2 Nephi 5)

The Division of the Nephites and Lamanites: A Lesson in Identity and Destiny

(2 Nephi 5)

In a pivotal moment that would forever shape the course of two civilizations, the Nephites and Lamanites find themselves at an impasse, leading to a separation that is as much about ideology as it is about lineage. This division, chronicled in the early chapters of 2 Nephi, isn't just a historical footnote; it's a profound narrative on the consequences of choices, beliefs, and the formation of identity—themes that deeply resonate with Generation Z.

The separation stems from fundamental disagreements and conflicts, underscoring the impact of values, visions for the future, and leadership on communal harmony. For young people today, living in a world often divided by ideologies and identities, this story highlights the importance of understanding, tolerance, and the quest for common ground. It serves as a cautionary tale about the long-term consequences of division and the potential for misunderstanding to breed discord and estrangement.

However, beyond the narrative of conflict, the separation of the Nephites and Lamanites also speaks to the formation of cultural identity and the ways communities rally around shared beliefs, values, and visions for the future. For Gen Z, navigating their personal and collective identities in a hyper-connected yet fragmented world, this story offers insights into the power of unity and the strength found in diversity.

The aftermath of the separation, where the Nephites establish a society based on their values and laws, and the Lamanites follow a different path, prompts reflection on the choices that define us. It challenges young individuals to consider how their beliefs and actions contribute to the communities they are part of and the kind of legacy they wish to leave.

Moreover, the narrative invites a discussion on reconciliation and understanding. It encourages today's youth to look beyond surface differences, to seek the humanity in everyone, and to work towards bridging divides through empathy, dialogue, and mutual respect.

Enos's Transformation: The Power of Earnest Prayer

(Enos 1)

Enos's Transformation: The Power of Earnest Prayer

(Enos 1)

In the quiet solitude of the wilderness, Enos, a young man carrying the weight of tradition and expectation, experiences a profound spiritual awakening that reshapes his understanding of faith, repentance, and divine communication. This moment of transformation begins with something deeply personal yet universally understood: a fervent prayer. It's a narrative that resonates strongly with Generation Z, a cohort navigating their spiritual and existential quests in an increasingly complex world.

Enos's story is not just about the act of praying but about the earnestness and sincerity behind it. In a digital age where communication is often reduced to quick texts and fleeting social media interactions, Enos's deep, contemplative dialogue with the divine stands as a testament to the power of genuine connection. His hours-long conversation with God reflects a level of dedication and introspection that invites young readers to consider the depth of their convictions and the nature of their own prayers.

The transformation Enos undergoes is profound. He receives not only the assurance of his forgiveness but also a heightened sense of responsibility towards his people and an unshakeable desire to serve them. This shift from personal salvation to communal concern mirrors the journey many young people today are on—moving from individualism to a more inclusive view of their role in society. Enos's story underscores the idea that true enlightenment comes with a commitment to the welfare of others, a message that aligns with the values of social justice and community service that are important to Generation Z.

Moreover, Enos's narrative is a powerful reminder of the potential for change within each person. It challenges the notion that one's past defines their future, offering hope and encouragement to those seeking redemption or a new path in life. It speaks to the capacity for inner transformation through sincere effort and divine grace, highlighting the importance of perseverance, faith, and the willingness to reach out in vulnerability.

For Generation Z, living in an era where authenticity and purpose are highly valued, Enos's experience with prayer provides a blueprint for spiritual exploration and personal growth. It invites young readers to engage in their spiritual journey with honesty and fervor, encouraging them to seek answers to their deepest questions and to be open to the transformative power of earnest communication with the divine.

King Benjamin's Teachings: A Blueprint for Service and Unity

(Mosiah 2-5)

King Benjamin's Teachings: A Blueprint for Service and Unity

(Mosiah 2-5)

In an era where leadership is often scrutinized through the lens of impact and ethical governance, King Benjamin's address to his people stands out as a timeless example of servant leadership and communal responsibility. Addressing his people one last time, King Benjamin doesn't just speak to them; he connects on a profound level, emphasizing service, humility, and the welfare of the community over personal gain. This message resonates deeply with Generation Z, a group characterized by their desire for authenticity, social justice, and meaningful change.

King Benjamin's teachings pivot around several core principles that echo the concerns and aspirations of young people today. Firstly, his emphasis on service to others as the foundation of a meaningful life challenges the individualistic tendencies of modern society. In a world where success is often measured by personal achievements and material wealth, King Benjamin reminds us of the fulfillment found in helping others and contributing to the community's well-being. This principle encourages young individuals to engage in acts of service, recognizing that true happiness and contentment come from lifting others.

Moreover, King Benjamin's discourse on equality and the eradication of class distinctions speaks directly to the heart of Generation Z's advocacy for social justice and equity. His call to view all individuals as equals, deserving of love and compassion, underscores the importance of dismantling systemic barriers and prejudices that divide society. It's a call to action for young people to lead the charge in creating a more inclusive and fair world.

Additionally, King Benjamin's teachings on humility and the acknowledgment of one's dependence on God for everything provide a counter-narrative to the self-aggrandizing culture prevalent on social media. It's a reminder of the value of humility and gratitude, virtues that foster a sense of community and shared destiny.

King Benjamin's address culminates in a collective covenant among his people to follow these principles, highlighting the power of unity in achieving societal transformation. For Generation Z, this story illustrates the impact of collective action guided by shared values and goals. It's an invitation to be part of something greater, to contribute to the building of a community grounded in service, compassion, and mutual respect.

King Noah's Downfall and Abinadi's Courage:
A Call for Integrity and Reform

(Mosiah 11-17)

King Noah's Downfall and Abinadi's Courage: A Call for Integrity and Reform
(Mosiah 11-17)

In the dramatic account of King Noah's reign and the prophetic admonitions of Abinadi, we find a compelling narrative of corruption, courage, and the unyielding power of truth. This story, set against the backdrop of a society led astray by its leaders, speaks volumes to Generation Z—a generation deeply invested in the ideals of transparency, accountability, and social reform.

King Noah, characterized by his greed, vanity, and disregard for the spiritual welfare of his people, represents the antithesis of ethical leadership. His actions, driven by self-interest and indulgence, lead to the moral and social decay of his community. In stark contrast, Abinadi emerges as a figure of integrity and bravery, standing alone to call out the corruption and to advocate for a return to righteousness. His willingness to speak truth to power, even at the cost of his life, underscores the importance of conviction and the impact of a single voice in challenging injustice.

For Generation Z, witnessing a global landscape marked by political turmoil and the fight for social justice, Abinadi's story resonates as a powerful example of individual activism. It highlights the role each person can play in advocating for change, emphasizing that standing up for what is right, even in the face of overwhelming opposition, can illuminate the path toward transformation.

Furthermore, the narrative explores the consequences of leadership that prioritizes personal gain over the common good. It serves as a cautionary tale about the long-term effects of corruption, urging young people to demand more from their leaders and to strive for positions of influence themselves, armed with integrity and a commitment to serving others.

Abinadi's unwavering faith and his ultimate sacrifice for his beliefs also speak to the concept of moral courage. It inspires young readers to consider their values and the lengths they are willing to go to defend them. In a culture often dominated by relativism and the fear of standing out, Abinadi's example encourages Generation Z to embrace their convictions with courage and to be agents of change in their communities.

Alma the Elder's Flight and the Church in the Wilderness

(Mosiah 18)

Alma the Elder's Flight and the Church in the Wilderness

(Mosiah 18)

In the midst of oppression under King Noah's unjust rule, Alma the Elder's transformation from a royal court member to a leader of spiritual renewal is a striking narrative of courage, faith, and community building. His flight into the wilderness, following his conversion through the teachings of Abinadi, and the subsequent establishment of a church based on the principles of kindness, equality, and mutual support offers a powerful blueprint for meaningful social engagement and collective action that resonates deeply with Generation Z.

Alma's story begins with a profound personal awakening, a moment of clarity that shifts his path from complicity in corruption to a courageous stand for truth and righteousness. This moment of conversion is emblematic of the journey many young people undertake today, seeking authenticity and purpose in a world that often values appearance over substance. Alma's decision to flee King Noah's tyrannical regime and create a community founded on different values is a testament to the power of change starting with individual conviction.

The establishment of the church in the wilderness by Alma is particularly significant. In a place devoid of societal structures, Alma and his followers create a space where spiritual and communal welfare takes precedence. The principles he instills—bearing one another's burdens, mourning with those who mourn, and standing as witnesses of God—echo the values of empathy, community service, and advocacy that are hallmarks of Generation Z's ethos. In a time when social isolation and division are prevalent, Alma's community represents an ideal of unity and support.

Furthermore, Alma's initiative to baptize his followers in the waters of Mormon, marking their commitment to their faith and to each other, symbolizes the transformative power of shared rituals and values in creating a cohesive community. For young people today, who often forge communities online and strive for social impact, the story of Alma's church offers insights into the importance of face-to-face connection, shared purpose, and collective action in effecting change.

Alma the Elder's narrative is a call to Generation Z to envision new forms of community and leadership that transcend traditional hierarchies and are rooted in principles of equality, compassion, and shared responsibility. It encourages young people to take bold steps in pursuit of their beliefs, to create spaces of inclusivity and support, and to engage in acts of service that uplift and unite.

The Transformation of Alma the Younger and the Sons of Mosiah

(Mosiah 27, Alma 36)

The Transformation of Alma the Younger and the Sons of Mosiah

(Mosiah 27, Alma 36)

In an age where stories of personal transformation and redemption resonate deeply, the dramatic conversion of Alma the Younger and the sons of Mosiah stands as a testament to the profound impact of second chances and the power of change. This narrative, rich with themes of forgiveness, enlightenment, and purpose, speaks volumes to Generation Z, a cohort deeply engaged in discussions about growth, identity, and the journey towards understanding one's true self.

Initially, Alma the Younger and the sons of Mosiah are depicted as rebellious figures, actively working against the beliefs and teachings of their community and their fathers. Their story mirrors the journey of many young people today, who may find themselves at odds with established norms, searching for meaning in a world saturated with conflicting messages. Their initial path, marked by defiance and dissent, is not unlike the process of questioning and exploration that many undergo in their quest to define their personal beliefs and values.

The turning point for Alma and his friends—a divine intervention that leads to a period of introspection and profound spiritual awakening—highlights the transformative power of confronting one's beliefs and actions. This moment of reckoning, where Alma is struck with the realization of his wrongdoings and the potential for change, underscores the theme of personal accountability and the possibility for redemption. It's a powerful reminder that change is possible, and that it's never too late to alter one's course and seek a life of purpose and integrity.

Post-conversion, the commitment of Alma and the sons of Mosiah to spread the message of change and to dedicate their lives to the service of others illustrates the potential for transformed individuals to effect positive change in their communities. Their journey from persecution to proclamation is emblematic of the belief that the most profound testimonies can come from the most unexpected sources, encouraging young individuals to recognize the value of their voices and experiences in advocating for truth and justice.

Alma and Amulek's Mission:
Unity in Adversity

(Mosiah 27, Alma 17-26)

Alma and Amulek's Mission: Unity in Adversity

(Mosiah 27, Alma 17-26)

In a society where the noise of division drowns out calls for change, the mission of Alma the Younger and Amulek emerges as a beacon of hope and determination. Their story, set against the backdrop of skepticism and resistance, highlights the profound impact of steadfast belief and the power of collaboration in the face of adversity.

Tasked with a divine mission to guide the lost back to the fold, Alma and Amulek faced not just external opposition but also internal trials that tested their faith to its core. Their journey is a testament to the resilience required to champion truth and righteousness in a world reluctant to embrace change. It's a narrative that resonates with today's youth, who are all too familiar with the challenges of advocating for justice and truth in an often indifferent society.

Yet, the essence of their story lies not in the obstacles they encountered but in their unyielding commitment to their cause and each other. Their partnership, strengthened by trials and shared convictions, exemplifies the notion that unity can forge paths through the most daunting barriers. This message of solidarity and mutual support offers a powerful lesson for Generation Z, emphasizing the importance of coming together to affect meaningful change.

Through their mission, Alma and Amulek inspired a movement of transformation, changing hearts and reshaping society. Their story serves as a reminder that even in the face of great opposition, courage, and collaboration can catalyze a ripple effect of positive change, echoing the potential within each individual to contribute to a larger narrative of progress and unity.

The Journey of Mosiah with the Golden Plates

(Mosiah 28, Alma 37)

The Journey of Mosiah with the Golden Plates

(Mosiah 28, Alma 37)

In an epic quest that combines the pursuit of knowledge with the essence of divine guardianship, the journey of Mosiah to secure the twenty-four golden plates is a riveting tale of discovery, responsibility, and the passing of wisdom across generations. This narrative holds particular significance, not only for its historical and spiritual revelations but also for its embodiment of the quest for understanding and the stewardship of truth.

Mosiah's expedition to obtain the plates is driven by a desire to preserve the history and teachings of his people for future generations. This mission, fraught with challenges and imbued with a sense of sacred duty, mirrors the contemporary journey of young individuals seeking to uncover and safeguard truths in a world often overshadowed by misinformation and fleeting attention spans.

The golden plates, containing the records of a civilization and the profound insights of prophets, symbolize the weight of knowledge and the importance of its preservation. Mosiah's commitment to securing these plates highlights the value of historical consciousness and the role it plays in shaping identity and guiding future actions. For Generation Z, living in an era of rapid information exchange, this story underscores the importance of discerning and preserving essential truths amidst the noise.

Furthermore, the transfer of the plates from Mosiah to Alma, and Alma's subsequent instruction to his son Helaman about their care and significance, encapsulates the principle of generational legacy. It emphasizes the responsibility of each generation to pass on knowledge and wisdom, ensuring that the lessons of the past inform the decisions of the future. This aspect of the narrative resonates with the modern emphasis on mentorship, sustainability, and the long-term impact of our actions on subsequent generations.

Nephite Judges: Democracy in Action

(Mosiah 29)

Nephite Judges:
Democracy in Action

(Mosiah 29)

Mosiah's bold decision to replace monarchy with a system of judges marks a foundational shift towards democracy in Nephite society. This move, driven by a desire to prevent corruption and power abuse, introduced a new era of governance where justice, accountability, and the voice of the people were paramount.

For Generation Z, witnessing today's political challenges, Mosiah's reforms highlight the importance of fair governance and the role of individuals in shaping their societies. It's a reminder that engagement and vigilance are crucial in maintaining a just system where leaders serve the common good.

This story champions the principles of democratic governance, urging young people to participate actively in their communities and to advocate for transparency and equity in leadership. It's a call to ensure that power remains in the hands of the people, safeguarding society from the pitfalls of unchecked authority.

In essence, Mosiah's establishment of judges is a timeless lesson on the value of democracy and the continuous effort required to sustain it, inspiring Generation Z to contribute to a fairer and more accountable society.

Chief Judge Alma's Reforms: Leadership and Justice

(Alma 1-4)

Chief Judge Alma's Reforms: Leadership and Justice

(Alma 1-4)

Alma's assumption of the role as the first chief judge in Nephite history was a moment of significant change, emphasizing the themes of moral leadership and societal reform. His efforts to establish justice and fairness, while combating the rise of dissent and inequality, reflect a deep commitment to the principles that underpin a stable and just society.

For Generation Z, living in an era where ethical leadership and social justice are central concerns, Alma's story resonates as an example of the impact that committed and principled leadership can have on society. His reforms highlight the importance of striving for equity and the role of leaders in guiding their communities toward these ideals.

This narrative encourages young individuals to seek out and support leaders who prioritize the welfare of all members of society and to recognize their responsibility in fostering a just and equitable community. It serves as a call to action for Generation Z to be agents of change in their own right, advocating for fairness and integrity in all areas of governance and society.

In summary, Alma's introduction as chief judge and his subsequent reforms offer a powerful lesson on the importance of leadership that is grounded in justice and the ongoing effort to create a society that reflects these values, inspiring young people to play an active role in shaping a fair and just world.

Zeezrom's Change:
Embracing Truth

(Alma 14-15)

Zeezrom's Change: Embracing Truth

(Alma 14-15)

Zeezrom's story is a compelling account of transformation, showcasing how a skeptic becomes a believer, illustrating the profound impact of facing one's doubts and embracing truth. Initially opposing Alma and Amulek with skepticism, Zeezrom represents the journey from questioning to understanding, from doubt to faith. His transformation begins as he genuinely engages with the teachings he once challenged, leading to a dramatic change in heart and mind.

This narrative resonates with Generation Z's experiences of navigating a world filled with conflicting information and viewpoints. Zeezrom's story encourages young individuals to approach their questions and doubts with openness, highlighting the importance of personal growth and the willingness to change one's perspective.

In essence, Zeezrom's journey from doubter to disciple underscores the value of seeking truth and the power of personal transformation. It's a reminder that change and understanding are possible for anyone willing to question, listen, and embrace new truths, offering inspiration for those on their paths of discovery and growth.

Ammon's Service
Among the Lamanites

(Alma 17-19)

Ammon's Service Among the Lamanites

(Alma 17-19)

Ammon's mission to the Lamanites, particularly his service to King Lamoni, is a compelling tale of dedication, understanding, and the transformative power of compassion. Venturing into potentially hostile territory, Ammon chooses to serve rather than preach initially, winning hearts through acts of kindness and unparalleled service. His approach, culminating in the miraculous conversion of King Lamoni and his court, underscores the profound impact of empathy and genuine human connection.

For Generation Z, living in an era where social divides seem more pronounced, Ammon's story is a beacon of hope. It exemplifies how barriers between people can be broken down through service and understanding. Ammon's willingness to connect on a human level, even with those considered adversaries, serves as a powerful model for bridging divides and fostering unity in diverse communities.

This narrative is a vivid reminder that real change often begins with the simple act of showing up and offering one's abilities for the betterment of others. Ammon's story encourages young individuals to look beyond surface differences, engage in acts of service, and embrace the potential within every person to change and grow. It's a call to action for empathy, patience, and the kind of leadership that serves first.

Ammon and His Brothers: Bridging Divides Through Faith

(Alma 17-27)

Ammon and His Brothers: Bridging Divides Through Faith

(Alma 17-27)

Ammon and his brothers' mission to the Lamanites is a profound narrative of courage, faith, and the power of reconciliation. Venturing into a land where they were unwelcome, they embarked on a journey not just to convert but to understand and connect with a people long considered enemies. Their approach, marked by humility and genuine love, led to the conversion of many Lamanites, transforming communities and bridging centuries-old divides.

For Generation Z, a group deeply concerned with social justice and unity, this story emphasizes the importance of empathy and open-hearted dialogue in overcoming prejudice and misunderstanding. It showcases how patience, compassion, and steadfastness in one's beliefs can lead to unexpected friendships and the breaking down of barriers.

Ammon and his brothers' experiences teach that true change comes from within and often requires a willingness to see the world from others' perspectives. Their story is a call to young people today to approach divisions with a mindset of healing and reconciliation, demonstrating that even the deepest divides can be bridged through faith, love, and understanding.

King Lamoni's Miraculous Conversion: A Tale of Insight and Transformation

(Alma 18-20)

King Lamoni's Miraculous Conversion: A Tale of Insight and Transformation

(Alma 18-20)

King Lamoni's conversion is a captivating story of enlightenment and change, sparked by the unlikely friendship between a king and a missionary, Ammon. Lamoni, initially intrigued by Ammon's dedication and power, finds himself questioning the very foundations of his beliefs. Through sincere dialogue and miraculous events, Lamoni experiences a profound spiritual awakening, leading to a transformation that not only alters his life but also impacts his entire kingdom.

This narrative is particularly relevant to Generation Z, emphasizing the power of personal connections and the potential for transformative insight when we're open to new perspectives. Lamoni's story illustrates that understanding and change often come from engaging with individuals who challenge our views, encouraging a willingness to explore deep questions and seek truth.

Lamoni's miraculous conversion reminds young individuals of the impact one person can have on another's life and, by extension, on broader communities. It champions the idea that empathy, open-mindedness, and the courage to embrace new truths can lead to significant personal and communal growth, inspiring young people to be catalysts for positive change in their own circles and beyond.

Aaron's Preaching
to King Lamoni's Father:
Understanding Beyond
Boundaries
(Alma 22)

Aaron's Preaching to King Lamoni's Father: Understanding Beyond Boundaries

(Alma 22)

Aaron's mission to King Lamoni's father showcases a pivotal moment of cross-cultural understanding and spiritual awakening. As Aaron steps into the realm of a king with deeply entrenched beliefs, he navigates the challenge with respect, patience, and clarity. The king, moved by Aaron's sincerity and the profound truths he shares, embarks on a personal journey of discovery that leads to a remarkable conversion and a commitment to spread the newfound faith across his lands.

This story resonates with Generation Z, highlighting the importance of respectful dialogue and the power of empathy in bridging divides. It demonstrates that profound understanding and transformation are possible when we approach one another with open hearts and minds, willing to share and learn from our diverse experiences.

Aaron's successful mission encourages young individuals to seek common ground, even in the face of seemingly insurmountable differences. It's a testament to the idea that genuine communication and the sharing of personal convictions can inspire change, not just on an individual level but across communities, fostering a more inclusive and understanding world.

The Story of
the Anti-Nefi-Lehis:
A Commitment to Peace

(Alma 23-24)

The Story of the Anti-Nefi-Lehis: A Commitment to Peace

(Alma 23-24)

The transformation of the Anti-Nefi-Lehis, who vow never to take up arms again, even in the face of potential annihilation, is a powerful narrative of conviction, peace, and forgiveness. Their decision to bury their weapons as a symbol of their commitment to nonviolence is a profound testament to the strength of their faith and their desire to live in harmony, regardless of the consequences.

For Generation Z, deeply engaged in global issues and the pursuit of peace, this story underscores the importance of steadfast principles and the courage it takes to stand by them, even when faced with significant risks. The Anti-Nefi-Lehis' choice to embrace peace, despite their turbulent past, serves as a compelling example of transformative justice and the potential for societal change through collective action and commitment to nonviolence.

This narrative invites young individuals to reflect on the power of collective peace commitments and the impact they can have on creating a more just and peaceful world. It challenges them to consider the values they stand for and how those values can be enacted in ways that foster reconciliation and understanding, encouraging a move towards actions that promote unity and healing.

The Debate Between
Alma and Korihor:
A Clash of Beliefs

(Alma 30)

The Debate Between Alma and Korihor: A Clash of Beliefs

(Alma 30)

In the engaging encounter between Alma and Korihor, the Nephite record presents a riveting dialogue that delves into faith, skepticism, and the nature of belief. Korihor, the self-proclaimed anti-Christ, challenges the foundational beliefs of Alma and his people, advocating for a perspective grounded in what he perceives as rational thought and observable evidence. Alma's response, rich in patience and insight, offers a defense not just of his faith but of the value of spiritual experience as a form of knowledge.

This story captures a moment of profound philosophical debate that resonates with Generation Z, a cohort often navigating the intersection of faith, science, and personal belief in an increasingly secular world. The discourse between Alma and Korihor invites young individuals to ponder the complexities of belief systems and the importance of respecting differing viewpoints while holding fast to one's convictions.

The resolution of the debate, where Korihor is ultimately confronted with the consequences of his unbelief, serves as a narrative exploration of the limits of skepticism and the potential pitfalls of denying the spiritual dimension of human experience. It underscores the idea that true understanding requires an openness to various forms of knowledge, including those that transcend empirical evidence.

For today's youth, the story of Alma and Korihor is a compelling reminder of the value of engaging with challenging ideas, the importance of spiritual introspection, and the power of faith as a guiding force in navigating the complexities of the modern world. It encourages a thoughtful examination of one's beliefs and an appreciation for the diverse ways in which truth and knowledge can manifest.

Alma and Ammon
Among the Zoramites:
Faith, Humility, and Inclusion
(Alma 31-34)

Alma and Ammon Among the Zoramites: Faith, Humility, and Inclusion

(Alma 31-34)

In their mission to the Zoramites, Alma the Younger and Ammon confront a society entrenched in spiritual elitism and ritualistic complacency. The Zoramites' prayer on the Rameumptom, a symbol of their exclusivity and pride, starkly contrasts with Alma and Ammon's teachings of humility, sincere prayer, and the inclusivity of God's love. Their efforts to bring the Zoramites back to a more heartfelt and inclusive faith underscore the importance of genuine spiritual connection over hollow rituals.

This narrative is especially relevant to Generation Z, a generation that values authenticity and inclusivity. It highlights the dangers of spiritual arrogance and the significance of creating communities where everyone feels welcomed and valued. Alma's and Ammon's teachings about the simplicity of faith and the power of sincere prayer resonate as a call to look beyond outward practices and find a deeper, more personal connection to faith and community.

The story of their mission is a reminder of the transformative power of humility and the importance of reaching out to those who feel marginalized or forgotten. It challenges young individuals to consider how they can foster environments of acceptance and understanding, both spiritually and in broader society.

Alma's Counsel
to His Son Helaman:
Wisdom Across Generations

(Alma 36-37)

Alma's Counsel to His Son Helaman: Wisdom Across Generations

(Alma 36-37)

In his heartfelt discourse to his son Helaman, Alma the Younger shares not only his most transformative personal experience—the moment of his own spiritual awakening—but also imparts wisdom and guidance for leading a life of integrity and purpose. He recounts his journey from rebellion to redemption, emphasizing the power of repentance and the mercy of God. This narrative is rich with lessons on the importance of learning from one's past, the value of sacred trusts, and the critical role of the scriptures in guiding one's life.

For Generation Z, this exchange between father and son highlights the timeless relevance of intergenerational wisdom and the importance of personal conviction. Alma's story encourages young people to seek their paths with courage, to embrace their own processes of learning and growth, and to value the wisdom passed down from previous generations.

Alma's counsel to Helaman about the responsibility of safeguarding and using the sacred records underscores the theme of stewardship over one's heritage and the knowledge that shapes our understanding of the world. It's a call to appreciate and preserve the wisdom of the past while applying it to the challenges of the present and the future.

This narrative invites young individuals to reflect on their own lives, to recognize the transformative power of genuine repentance, and to understand the importance of making choices that align with their deepest values. It serves as a reminder that each person's journey is unique and that true wisdom comes from applying the lessons of the past with an eye towards creating a better future.

Shiblon's Steadfastness: From Rebellion to Redemption

(Alma 38)

Shiblon's Steadfastness: From Rebellion to Redemption

(Alma 38)

In his address to Shiblon, Alma the Younger acknowledges his son's past rebellion, yet focuses on Shiblon's remarkable transformation and steadfastness in the face of adversity. This account not only celebrates Shiblon's redemption but also emphasizes the virtues of patience, courage, and humility. Alma commends Shiblon for his endurance and for the example he has set, illustrating the profound impact of personal change and resilience.

For Generation Z, Shiblon's story resonates as a powerful example of personal growth and the capacity to evolve beyond past mistakes. It underscores the importance of facing challenges with fortitude and finding strength in one's convictions. Alma's praise for Shiblon's humility and service to others highlights the value placed on empathy and the positive influence one can have on those around them.

This narrative encourages young individuals to embrace their journeys of self-discovery and growth, recognizing that true character is forged in the crucible of life's challenges. Shiblon's transformation and the recognition he receives from his father serve as reminders that redemption is always within reach and that steadfastness in the face of adversity is a virtue to be cherished and nurtured.

Alma's Counsel to Corianton: Guidance on Repentance and Redemption
(Alma 39-42)

Alma's Counsel to Corianton: Guidance on Repentance and Redemption

(Alma 39-42)

Alma's heartfelt counsel to his son Corianton, who strayed from his duties and moral path, unfolds as a profound discussion on the consequences of actions, the process of repentance, and the overarching plan of redemption. Through this dialogue, Alma addresses Corianton's missteps, not with condemnation but with a father's deep concern and a desire to guide his son back to righteousness. This sermon encapsulates themes of accountability, forgiveness, and the enduring love and mercy of God.

For Generation Z, Alma's approach offers a compelling model for addressing personal and moral failures—highlighting the importance of understanding the impact of our choices while emphasizing the potential for growth and learning from our mistakes. Alma's detailed explanation of the plan of salvation and the principles of justice and mercy provides a rich theological framework that reassures Corianton—and by extension, all readers—that despite our flaws, there is always a path to improvement and redemption.

This narrative is especially relevant today, as it encourages open dialogue about ethical living and personal integrity. It reminds young individuals of the value of self-reflection and the power of change, reinforcing the message that it's never too late to correct our course and strive for a higher standard of conduct.

The Nephite Wars: Lessons in Courage and Conviction
(Alma 43-62)

The Nephite Wars:
Lessons in Courage and Conviction

(Alma 43-62)

The protracted conflicts between the Nephites and the Amalickiahites encapsulate a period of intense struggle, not only on the battlefield but also in the hearts and minds of those fighting for their homes, families, and freedoms. These chapters narrate the complexities of war, the strategies employed by both sides, and the profound acts of bravery and sacrifice exhibited by leaders like Captain Moroni and his soldiers. Through these accounts, themes of loyalty, moral integrity, and the costs of preserving freedom and righteousness emerge.

For Generation Z, a generation engaged with global issues of justice and peace, these narratives offer powerful reflections on the nature of conflict and the principles worth defending. The story of the Title of Liberty, a symbol raised by Captain Moroni to rally his people in defense of their faith, families, and freedoms, resonates as a call to stand firm in the face of adversity for causes that transcend individual interests.

These chapters also explore the personal sacrifices made by those committed to defending their society's values, highlighting the balance between aggression and defense, and the importance of ethical leadership in times of crisis. The resilience and strategic ingenuity displayed by the Nephites in their defense against aggressors provide lessons in overcoming challenges through unity, strategy, and faith.

For today's youth, the Nephite wars underscore the importance of understanding the causes and consequences of conflicts and the significance of working towards peace and justice. It encourages a critical examination of what it means to fight for righteous causes and the importance of standing up for one's beliefs, even in the face of overwhelming odds.

Nephi and Lehi's Mission Among the Lamanites: A Story of Faith and Miracles

(Helaman 5)

Nephi and Lehi's Mission Among the Lamanites: A Story of Faith and Miracles

(Helaman 5)

In Helaman 5, the mission of Nephi and Lehi, the sons of Helaman, to the Lamanites is a compelling narrative of faith, divine intervention, and the unifying power of God's love. Venturing into potentially hostile territory, they are driven by a profound commitment to share their beliefs and bring about spiritual awakening among the Lamanites. Their journey is marked by significant challenges, including imprisonment, yet it culminates in miraculous events that not only lead to their miraculous deliverance but also to the conversion of many Lamanites.

This story resonates with Generation Z by illustrating the transformative power of faith and the impact of standing firm in one's convictions, even in the face of adversity. The miraculous events surrounding Nephi and Lehi's mission–such as the appearance of a pillar of fire and a voice from heaven–emphasize that remarkable outcomes are possible when one is guided by faith and a genuine desire to benefit others.

The narrative also highlights the theme of reconciliation and unity across divides. The conversions that follow Nephi and Lehi's imprisonment bring together communities that were once estranged, showcasing the potential for understanding, forgiveness, and peace when hearts are changed.

For today's youth, Nephi and Lehi's mission is a powerful example of how steadfast belief, coupled with compassionate action, can bridge gaps and foster communal harmony. It encourages young individuals to consider how their own convictions can be a force for positive change and to approach challenges with the belief that faith and love can lead to unexpected and transformative outcomes.

Samuel the Lamanite's Prophecies: Warnings and Hope

(Helaman 13-16)

Samuel the Lamanite's Prophecies: Warnings and Hope

(Helaman 13-16)

Samuel the Lamanite stands atop the walls of Zarahemla, delivering a message that is both a dire warning and a beacon of hope. His prophecies, detailing the consequences of the Nephites' continued wickedness alongside the signs of Christ's birth and death, encapsulate the critical themes of accountability, repentance, and redemption. Samuel's unique position as an outsider speaking truth to power amplifies the urgency and poignancy of his message.

For Generation Z, Samuel's story is a compelling narrative about the courage it takes to speak out against prevailing injustices and the importance of heeding warnings about societal decline. His perseverance in the face of rejection and his commitment to delivering his message, despite personal risk, resonate with young activists today who are often at the forefront of calls for change.

Samuel's prophecies also serve as a reminder of the power of hope and the potential for renewal. His detailed predictions about the signs of Christ's coming offer a forward-looking perspective that encourages faith in future possibilities and the belief that light can emerge from darkness.

This narrative invites Generation Z to reflect on their role in addressing contemporary challenges, urging them to consider the long-term consequences of societal actions and the importance of striving for a better future. It highlights the value of listening to voices calling for change, especially those from marginalized or unexpected sources, and the transformative potential of embracing hope and working towards redemption.

The Revelation of
Christ's Birth to Nephi
(3 Nephi 1)

The Revelation of Christ's Birth to Nephi

(3 Nephi 1)

In 3 Nephi 1, as the long-anticipated sign of Christ's birth approaches, the Nephite society is fraught with tension and disbelief. Nephi, leading with steadfast faith amidst growing skepticism, fervently prays for a sign to reaffirm the prophecy's truth. The response—a night without darkness, signifying the Savior's birth—is a profound testament to God's faithfulness and the power of prayer. This moment not only strengthens the believers but also serves as a pivotal sign of hope and renewal for the entire Nephite nation.

For Generation Z, this narrative emphasizes the importance of faith and perseverance in times of doubt and fear. It showcases the impact of collective anticipation and the transformative power of witnessing a prophecy fulfilled. The revelation of Christ's birth to Nephi, and subsequently to all who witnessed the sign, underscores the theme that even in moments of great uncertainty, there are opportunities for reaffirmation of faith and deep spiritual awakening.

This story invites young individuals to reflect on the moments of darkness in their own lives and the world, encouraging them to seek out and recognize signs of hope and light. It illustrates that, through faith and prayer, it is possible to find reassurance and witness the unfolding of greater purposes, even when the future seems uncertain.

The Destruction at Nephite: Lessons from Calamity

(3 Nephi 8-10)

The Destruction at Nephite: Lessons from Calamity

(3 Nephi 8-10)

The cataclysmic events that engulf the Nephite lands following Christ's crucifixion are both a literal and metaphorical storm, marking a pivotal moment of destruction, reflection, and eventual divine communication. The intense darkness, natural disasters, and the voice of the Savior speaking from the darkness serve as powerful symbols of the consequences of societal neglect and spiritual waywardness, but also of God's enduring love and the potential for redemption.

For Generation Z, this narrative resonates on multiple levels, highlighting the fragility of societies and the environment, the importance of heeding warnings, and the need for collective repentance and change. It underscores the critical lesson that calamities, whether environmental, societal, or personal, call for introspection, humility, and a renewed commitment to living in harmony with divine principles.

The moments of silence that follow the destruction invite reflection on the impact of our actions on the world and each other, urging a reconsideration of priorities and values in light of potential consequences. Yet, the voice of Christ that pierces the darkness brings hope, offering forgiveness and a path forward for those willing to listen and change.

This story challenges young individuals to confront the realities of their world, to recognize the interconnectedness of all life, and to understand their role in fostering a just, sustainable, and compassionate society. It serves as a reminder that, even in the aftermath of tragedy, there is an opportunity for renewal and healing, if we are willing to turn towards the light of hope and embrace the principles of love and stewardship.

Christ's Teachings on Baptism, Faith, and Prayer

(3 Nephi 11-18)

Christ's Teachings on Baptism, Faith, and Prayer

(3 Nephi 11-18)

In the aftermath of tumult and darkness, the appearance of Jesus Christ among the Nephites opens a chapter of profound teaching and spiritual rejuvenation. His instructions on baptism, faith, and prayer lay the foundational stones for a renewed society, emphasizing the principles of unity, commitment, and direct communion with the divine. These teachings, delivered with compassion and authority, serve not only to guide the Nephites but to offer timeless wisdom for all who seek understanding and connection with God.

For Generation Z, Christ's teachings resonate as an invitation to explore the depths of their own faith, to understand the significance of sacred ordinances like baptism, and to appreciate the power of prayer as a means of personal and collective dialogue with the divine. In a world often characterized by division and distraction, the emphasis on faith and the unity achieved through baptism underscores the importance of community and shared spiritual journey.

Moreover, Christ's injunction to pray always and to seek the Father's will offers a model for living that is deeply rooted in mindfulness, compassion, and an ongoing quest for guidance and enlightenment. It encourages young individuals to see prayer not just as a ritual but as a vital practice for fostering connection, understanding, and peace in their lives.

These chapters from 3 Nephi invite Generation Z to reflect on their spiritual paths, to consider the transformative power of faith and the sacraments, and to embrace prayer as a profound source of strength, guidance, and comfort. It's a call to engage with spiritual principles in a manner that enriches personal growth and contributes to the well-being of the broader community.

Christ's Visit to the Americas: A Message of Peace and Unity

(3 Nephi 11-28)

Christ's Visit to the Americas: A Message of Peace and Unity

(3 Nephi 11-28)

The appearance of Jesus Christ in the Americas, following His resurrection, marks a pivotal moment of healing, instruction, and transformation. As He descends from the heavens and stands among the people, Christ brings a message of peace, love, and redemption, extending an invitation to come unto Him. Through His teachings, miracles, and the establishment of His church, He lays a foundation for a society based on compassion, unity, and divine principles.

For Generation Z, this narrative offers profound insights into the power of spiritual presence and the impact of living according to higher truths. Christ's visit underscores the importance of forgiveness, the value of small acts of kindness, and the potential for collective harmony when individuals embrace love as the guiding force in their lives. His teachings on prayer, faith, and the Beatitudes provide a blueprint for building a life of spiritual depth and purpose.

Moreover, Christ's blessing of the children and His healing of the sick highlight the themes of innocence and the transformative power of faith and compassion. These moments resonate with young individuals today, emphasizing that everyone has a role in fostering a community where care and attention to the vulnerable are paramount.

This account also presents a model of how diverse groups can come together in moments of shared spiritual experience, breaking down barriers and fostering a sense of common humanity. It challenges Generation Z to consider how they can contribute to a society where peace and mutual respect prevail, inspired by the ideals presented in Christ's teachings.

Christ's Sermon on
the Mount in the Americas

(3 Nephi 12-14)

Christ's Sermon on the Mount in the Americas

(3 Nephi 12-14)

When Jesus Christ delivers the Sermon on the Mount to the Nephites, He reiterates and expands upon the teachings He once shared in Jerusalem, tailoring His message to a people recovering from catastrophe and looking for guidance. This sermon, with its beatitudes, counsel on prayer, fasting, and judgment, and the call to be perfect as the Father is perfect, lays out a comprehensive guide for living a life that is spiritually fulfilling and morally sound.

For Generation Z, navigating a complex world of moral ambiguities and seeking authenticity, Christ's teachings in these chapters offer timeless wisdom on how to live with integrity and purpose. The beatitudes, blessings for those who embody qualities like meekness, mercy, and peacemaking, highlight the value of virtues that are often overlooked in today's success-driven culture. They serve as a reminder that true strength and happiness come from character, compassion, and a commitment to doing what is right.

Christ's emphasis on the importance of inner purity over outward show, as well as His call to love our enemies and to forgive others, challenges young individuals to look beyond societal norms and to cultivate a heart that reflects divine love and understanding. His teachings invite reflection on personal attitudes and actions, encouraging a shift towards more meaningful, empathetic interactions with the world.

The peaceful World
(4 Nephi 1)

The peaceful World

(4 Nephi 1)

In 4 Nephi 1, we're presented with an inspiring account of a society that achieved an unparalleled era of peace and unity following Christ's visit to the Americas. This chapter details the transformation of the Nephites and Lamanites, who, having been touched by the teachings of Jesus, dissolve their long-standing divisions to create a harmonious community based on principles of equality, love, and shared prosperity.

For 200 years, they live without contention, sharing all things in common, eliminating poverty, and embracing a collective identity that transcends previous enmities. Their society is characterized by remarkable achievements in peace, justice, and spiritual wellbeing, providing a profound example of what is possible when individuals are united in their commitment to live according to Christ's teachings.

This narrative is particularly resonant for Generation Z, a cohort deeply concerned with issues of social justice, equality, and community wellbeing. The story of 4 Nephi 1 offers a visionary example of a society that mirrors many of the ideals young people today are striving to realize. It highlights the transformative impact of shared values and collective action in overcoming societal divisions and creating an environment where everyone can thrive.

The Journey of the Jaredites: From Babel to a New World

(Ether 1-6)

The Journey of the Jaredites: From Babel to a New World

(Ether 1-6)

The story of the Jaredites begins with their departure from the Tower of Babel, a time of great division among humankind, leading to a quest for a promised land under divine guidance. This epic tale, chronicled in the book of Ether, spans the Jaredites' preparation, their remarkable journey across the sea in specially constructed barges, and their arrival in the promised land. It's a narrative rich with themes of faith, innovation, and resilience.

The Jaredites' journey starts with the brother of Jared's fervent prayer to spare his people from the confusion of tongues at Babel. Their plea is answered, setting them on a path marked by divine interventions and miraculous guidance. The construction of the barges, illuminated by stones touched by the hand of God, symbolizes the blending of human effort with divine assistance, highlighting the importance of faith and ingenuity in overcoming challenges.

For Generation Z, the Jaredites' story resonates as an allegory of perseverance in the face of uncertainty and the power of innovation in solving seemingly insurmountable problems. Their journey across vast waters in vessels of their own making speaks to the spirit of exploration and the courage to venture into the unknown, guided by a belief in a better future.

Moreover, the narrative underscores the value of community and collective action. The Jaredites, moving together as a people towards a common goal, exemplify the strength found in unity and shared purpose. This aspect of the story encourages young individuals to consider how collaboration and faith in a collective vision can pave the way for achieving significant goals.

The Tower of Babel
and the Jaredites' Language
Preservation
(Ether 2)

The Tower of Babel and
the Jaredites' Language Preservation

(Ether 2)

In Ether 2, the narrative delves into the pivotal moment at the Tower of Babel, an event symbolizing human ambition clashing with divine will, leading to the dispersal of humanity through the confounding of languages. Amidst this chaos, the Jaredites stand as a beacon of unity and preservation. Their plea to God—to maintain their language intact—marks a profound moment of faith and divine intervention, allowing them not only to communicate seamlessly among themselves but also to carry their culture and identity into a new world.

This account offers Generation Z a perspective on the importance of language and communication as foundational pillars of community and identity. In an era where digital platforms create both connections and divisions, the story of the Jaredites emphasizes the power of a shared language to unite people and preserve cultural heritage.

Moreover, the episode at the Tower of Babel serves as a reflection on the consequences of unchecked ambition and the importance of aligning human endeavors with ethical considerations and divine principles. It prompts young individuals to contemplate the balance between progress and humility, urging a consideration of how their actions contribute to the collective well-being.

The preservation of the Jaredites' language and their subsequent journey to a promised land, guided by divine light, underscores themes of resilience, adaptability, and the pursuit of a higher purpose. For Generation Z, this narrative is a call to value their cultural and linguistic heritage, to foster unity in diversity, and to navigate the challenges of the modern world with faith and collective vision.

Moroni's Vision of
the Latter Days and
the Invitation to Chris
(Moroni 7-8, 10)

Moroni's Vision of the Latter Days and the Invitation to Chris

(Moroni 7-8, 10)

In Moroni 7-8 and 10, Moroni, addressing a future generation, shares profound insights and exhortations that bridge time and space. His teachings on faith, hope, charity, the innocence of children, and the necessity of coming unto Christ for salvation are pivotal. These chapters also include Moroni's challenge to seek divine verification of the truth through prayer with real intent, promising that the Holy Ghost will confirm the truth of the Book of Mormon to all who earnestly seek.

For Generation Z, living in an era marked by uncertainty and a quest for authenticity, Moroni's words resonate deeply. His discourse on the pure love of Christ (charity) and its supreme importance in the Christian life emphasizes the transformative power of love and the essential nature of empathy and compassion in our interactions. It's a call to cultivate qualities that foster genuine connections and contribute to a more loving and understanding world.

Moroni's teachings about the innocence of children and their inherent worth challenge young individuals to reflect on societal values and the respect afforded to the perspectives and rights of the youngest among us. It underscores the importance of nurturing a world where innocence is protected and valued.

Furthermore, Moroni's invitation to test the truthfulness of his words through prayer speaks directly to the desire for personal revelation and the importance of individual spiritual journeys. In a world crowded with information and competing voices, the promise that truth can be discerned through sincere prayer and the whisperings of the Holy Ghost offers a beacon of clarity and personal conviction.

Moroni's Promise:
A Guiding Light for
Seekers of Truth
(Moroni 10)

Moroni's Promise:
A Guiding Light for Seekers of Truth

(Moroni 10)

In the concluding chapter of the Book of Mormon, Moroni extends an invitation that has illuminated the path for millions seeking confirmation of the book's divine origins and truths. He promises that anyone who reads the Book of Mormon, ponders its messages in their heart, and then asks God with a sincere heart and real intent, believing in Christ, will receive a confirmation of its truth through the Holy Spirit. This promise is not just a testament to the book's veracity but a profound invitation to personal revelation and spiritual discovery.

For Generation Z, navigating a world rich with information yet craving genuine truth, Moroni's promise offers a compelling approach to finding answers. It emphasizes the power of personal prayer, the importance of earnest seeking, and the availability of divine guidance in our quest for understanding. This invitation to direct communication with the divine resonates with young individuals yearning for authentic experiences and personal connections with something greater than themselves.

Moroni's promise also underscores the principle that truth is accessible to all who genuinely seek it, irrespective of their background or current beliefs. It's a reminder that the journey toward truth is personal, that faith involves action, and that sincere questions directed towards God can lead to profound insights and spiritual assurance.

Moreover, Moroni's challenge to test the truthfulness of the Book of Mormon encourages a proactive stance towards spiritual learning, inviting Generation Z to engage deeply with the text and to seek their own spiritual confirmations. It reassures them that faith and reason can coexist, that spiritual truths can withstand scrutiny, and that divine light is available to illuminate their understanding.

Made in the USA
Las Vegas, NV
26 December 2024